SERIOUSLY

Jack Solloway is a writer from the West Midlands living in London. His poetry has appeared in *Poetry Birmingham Literary Journal* and *Poetry Wales*; his prose in *The London Magazine*, *TLS*, and *Modern Poetry in Translation* among others.

Also by Jack Solloway

Lyrical Ballads   (Legitimate Snack, 2022)

Seriously

Jack Solloway

Broken Sleep Books

ISBN: 978-1-915760-39-5

Cover designed by Aaron Kent

Edited and typeset by Aaron Kent

Broken Sleep Books Ltd
Rhydwen
Talgarreg
Ceredigion
SA44 4HB

Broken Sleep Books Ltd
Fair View
St Georges Road
Cornwall
PL26 7YH

Contents

My smiles must be sincere or not at all.

— Byron

It's just a bit of fun.

— Brydon

Ug

me watch
me fire build
me dream

Queen Mab

Great as the old back garden, the night,
A microbial patch of time, bewitches us.

Dream not of Mars, gods, or moonlight
But particles, all, a treacle of miniatures.

Atoms, in their silent ministry, ensnare
Our unseen world with desire's gravity.

Their elf-locked mischief is everywhere
At once, a braiding & uncombable sea.

It is night, fermenting love's sluttishness,
When secrets kept like stars come out.

A worm in the eye, this Queen Mab is—
When I miss you most she's always about.

Fancy dress
for Sacha

It's 2200, and the Noah's ark
bop just off the old High Street
is sexless, so I bail.

Giraffes was your idea, a pair
of Alice bands with little horns
erect, our tails pinned.

I've met piñatas more convincing.
But we are fit to burst and young
and dressed to match:

In short, you always stick your neck
out for me. On the town, a man
like a rain-drunk god

lashes down at us. He thinks he
spots a love-condemned animal
unsteady on their feet.

He thinks the cobbles after rain
are shiners, bright as fishbacks, slick
in the blue-black starlight.

When, really, Oxford's dry tonight.
There's Mesopotamia here, a little
field beside fresh water.

The flood plains never fill high
enough to drown acacia trees.
We are safe, you say.

I try to picture a large canopy,
an upturned shield or umbrella,
like a green coracle.

On better days I remember
the tall branches of the acacia.
The rest, it doesn't matter.

Cheeseburgers at the Met

The cheeseburgers at the Met are grass-fed
And draped in special sauce. What a serving!
House pickles, fries, extra extras on the side
Congesting my rib-cage for the rib-watchers.
Greta's alive, others not. Like it's news again.
In the caff behind the Lehman Wing, the art

Of the dollar slice is prized greater than art
By Dutch Masters. Blokes' still lives are fed
Up with soap-bubbles and tulips. Look again
At the bun grease, the eat-out trays serving
Nike-swoosh tourists, the shucked watchers
In their Wayfarer lenses, socket-black, side-

Eyeing, like anosmic snufflers, the underside
Of some West Fifty-fourth Street spread. Art
Loves it when you're dead. Grazing watchers
In cod-flesh socks and roll-necks are overfed.
I wonder if Hirst's formaldehyde-preserving
Tanks are haemorrhaging their guts again…

The burger's divine (like I'm in love again).
I forget her, limbs crossed, Cupid's ex side-
Piece, while romancing this $13.25 serving.
Kissing is eating without food, itself an art.
A pair canoodle by the fountain, penny-fed
By oxidised wishes. The queueing watchers

Drown a coin, cough, ignore other watchers.
Some wait centuries for a toilet. Back again
So soon? Food here's faster than you're fed.
Tastemakers, too. Clenching your backside,
You ogle the latest Rembrandt they call art.
Hope it brushes off. The real selfie's serving

Feather-in-his-cap, 'died a pauper', serving
No one. Heda's next. He turfs his watchers
Out of a decent meal. We arrive late to art,
Faces pecking perennially at the glass again
Of some lived interior. I'll meet you outside
The Met later, when it's time again to be fed.

How's 5ish? *Art was meh. Still, they're serving*
Burgers. Hawkish as a fed, I watch the watchers
Till I'm gone again, along the Upper East Side.

'Can birds do what they like?'

after Brian and Charles (2022)

The second-hand keyboard is patient,
A poor dentistry of smiles that knows the peril

Of local ambition from its makeshift perch on the sill.
The stand is with a writer. It's not mine

Yet. The little robot I borrowed makes sound
From sound, and walks along to Ornithology.

It imitates. It is an imitator. It is a cheap instrument
Like a washing machine for a stomach.

Like gloves for hands. Like your grandmother's curtains
I fashion for a dress. Or my first trip to the shops

For milk, old man in shoes, face like a found object
Whose repurposing makes a parent worried sick.

I play with automatic hand and think on the upward stair
Of you, like a banister at the contour of its spiral.

It's nice here. Tree outside the window. Dictionary at the door.
Playing pretend the lightning strike's amateur scientist.

You can call me Charles, if you like. It's the likeness that does
    it. He sounds just like a real person.

Social media

I would reply to you online
But wish I could correctly
I do not wish a foot gone wrong
For fear that you'll correct me

For fear it comes, it is not right
But wrong to paralyse
And makes a coward of intent
Called action in disguise

Called action? Well, I cannot say
Since I've not got the gumption
If writing's action (its true name)
Or derring-do assumption

And do I dare—Christ! Where'd you come from?
I shall be notified
The advert tolls and makes me dumb
With shame as if I lied

It's some relief when all's forgot
The message must be instant
The feed's gone dead and all's forgot
What is, is non-existent

My courage lives to fight again
Untouched but worse unliked
Perhaps I'll send my words to you
But oh what should I write

Metaverse

fuck
you , mark

Keel

I did a man for an odd sock
In a fit of recognition or absence of mind
I could not tell

His business was his own,
The sock of memorable colour
Situated like a pool
In the middle of Colmore Row

The man, we can get
A better look at him now,
He takes off his hat like a Stetson
And stoops forward into
An elderly shadow

I've closed the distance
To see he is a rich man,
Richer than me

An austere face
Neat, kind and timely
Fond in the familiar or relative way
Of two passing, kindred souls
Entangled

The sock is raggedy old, missing
A toe and scarcely
Fit for purpose
But he is not to have it

For I take off my shoe
From Marks & Spencer's 2-for-1 sale
And keel him like a god
Into a superposition

That another of us, say, in Paris or Beijing
Finds a doppled, matching pair in the self-
Same memorable colour
    One felled, shoe in hand   }
    One poised, sock in other   }
Is probably not incidental

There is no counterfactual
There is no causation or reprieve
There is nothing believable about this
    Because it is real   }
    Because it is true   }

Whenever I tell this story, everyone cheers and claps for
    miles around and is a viral sensation

i can't even
right now
said the sun
on his cloud
it's not even
half eleven

that's odd
said the moon
a fraction soon
whose prime
time waned
gone seven

In the House that Jack Built

there once was a shoe. foom-tchee foom-tchee. the shoe is there. foom-tchee foom-tchee. there once was a shoe that belongs to a foot, that foot is mine. foom-tchee foom-tchee. the shape of the foot. foom-tchee foom-tchee. has a gum and a tongue. foom-tchee foom-tchee. the shape of the foot has a gum and a tongue, is one foot long. foom-tchee foom-tchee. the length of the tongue. foom-tchee foom-tchee. is one foot long. foom-tchee foom-tchee. the length of the room on the length of the tongue is one foot long. foom-tchee foom-tchee. the tongue is yours. foom-tchee foom-tchee. the room's mine. foom-tchee foom-tchee. the love in the room at the foot of the bed by the shoes is ours. foom-tchee foom-tchee. the shoes are off. foom-tchee foom-tchee. it's three o'clock. foom-tchee foom-tchee. the shoes that are off with the tongue hanging out are open, unlaced. foom-tchee foom-tchee. here are the socks. foom-tchee foom-tchee. the shoes are sick. foom-tchee foom-tchee. the shoes that are sick and the socks that are hid in the shape of the shoe with the gum and the tongue that is one foot long are quietly rocked in the arms of the clock as the night peters out through the room, the room, the room, as night peters out through the room

Dodo

after Charles Dodgson

Whopping long-footed to the rhythm of a joke,
Like a mathematician's stutter, or double helix,
The sluggard expresses the improbable odds
Of a perfect answer to the question of the body.

Observe, the idiot bird, attentive Attenborough,
How no better actor of flesh and brood, though
Cannier, puppeteers along the Mauritian bank
These two legs, ripe belly, and wings for hands:

How it crosses the road, skims pebbles in the green
Shade, or else honeymoons in the lapsing ocean
Of a paradise sweeter than a default screensaver,
Full-knowing bliss, no strings attached, all inclusive.

So well abstracted this rustic booby's frolics are,
Whose pratting about, plain and simple, makes a shire
Of the whole wide island, from Siren to St Brandon,
Where no Dutchman's flying colours have yet landed,

That, evolved for leisure, it goes by an idle verb,
Making do twice over, a hopeful thing, still bird
But more balloon animal, inspired and end-tied
For a children's party where no clown was hired.

What a natural! Fruit-picker, model, bindlestiff,
Stone-swallowing carny, a free ranging talent, it
Swells like a peacock, broad native confidence,
Imperiously keeping on keeping up appearances

Long after the settler had lost reason to fly,
To play the costume of its past self, a parody.
But stop me if you've heard this one before,
About wonderous tales, worlds, ships at dawn,

As we, too, are stranded on the entangled bank,
With the turtle, the eaglet, the oyster and crab,
Metabolised from the same primordial soup,
A gonzo, not the naturalist we had presumed.

Night chases day, morning lunch, midday dinner,
As a matter of course. Am I accommodated here?
The mock-learnèd avian, eyes vacant and rolling,
Squats low, knot-arsed, on the point like an egg.

That's the way to do it, cries the nesting don,
With professorial swazzle, panto-like in tone,
His mottled feathers grey, bruised and dun
Standing on end as though awaiting applause.

The sun laughs the ground aghast of light,
The waves clap and roar, the creatures fit,
The palms bent double from shore to shore,
As the idiot bird, pleased as punch, bows.

Sails catching wind of the promise of Eden
Are not in on the prank, suggests the horizon,
The finish line invisible—the race is near run.
We're not far behind you. Dodo d-dodge, s—!

BBC commission

There's nothing poetic
About atopic eczema

Except perhaps the barrier
Missing between my skin

Everything and all it touches
Especially your shit poem

The hinge

my lover's cupboard has no handles
my lover's cupboard unmans me

my lover's cupboard has no handles
because I open at the hinge

my lover's cupboard's my opponent
my lover's cupboard's shut to me

my lover's cupboard's my opponent
because I open at the hinge

my lover's cupboard's built to purpose
my lover's cupboard's hers not mine

my lover's cupboard's built to purpose
because I open at the hinge

so if your cupboard has no handles
and my cupboard has no handles

and your cupboard has no handles
because I open at the hinge

ANAGRAM
— OF —

IN A STATION OF THE METRO

His abstract image of people beneath earth
plants too the distinct touch of rain;
O, awaken few.

ARDEN
2020.

I.
Dating

There are severed heads in the British Museum
The human kind if you'd like to see them
I can book a ticket
If you fancy it

O, it says here
They're not for display
But we can go there anyway

II.
Shave and a Haircut

In two bits

I'll pay a professional
To remove my hair
That I've earned
Which is mine

No, no, it's fine
I
  won't be
        taking
It home

Language games

'The weather is fine.'

— *Ludwig Wittgenstein*

When I say: the burdocks
        in the garden
               are grieving
You say: the condition for a choir of chairs is therapy

When I say: but they laugh in the sun
           and cry when it's gone
You say: solutions to the calendar year are marked
  on the fridge

When I say: the sky has
     help!   fallen in,
         help!
             help!
You say: a thought experiment our friends are over, and
  you've walked it through the carpet

When I say: the windows
        are toddlers
         catching droplets
     on their tongues
       like flies
You say: this flat is not a heath in the interest of comfort and
  security

When I say: I <u>am</u> a
     wandering cloud; I took
  a litmus test to understand
    my personality type
You say: the evidence is undeniable as chalk on the lawn

               When I say:

that is not what
    I meant that is not
      what I meant
      at all
               You say:

why not own your mistakes?
and anyway, it's no excuse it's
fucking wet in here

               When I say:
     look,   I am   water
  a pattern   dust   of   ice
     intention   comprising   vapour
       and   sea salt
You say:
    the living space is to be referred to the Hague

When I say: where the firmament,
   where the welkin, where the leaky vaults
  of heaven, lo! these three are my moods
You say: the terms of discussion are furniture,
  and you are <u>not</u> inevitable

When I say: believe me when I say:
    hurricanoes is a living picture of the
    permanent brain alighting from
    itself
You say:

          an overwritten sky
       hang it there on the wall

When I say: the terms of debate are not furniture, they mean
    the difference between you and I
                   You say: prove it.

I say: your eyes are soft-
    boiled bulbs on the
    electric stove; I go-
    uge them out
You say: the art of silence and agnosticism

I say: to crown
You say: no no what are you doing

I say: —
You say: oh my god my god my eyes

I say: the cliff
You say: my eyes my eyes Jack please I can't find the door

I say: jump
but with my hands
You say:
You say:
You say:

You say:

You say:

You say:

You say:

You say:

You say:

You say:

You say:

You say:

You say:

You say: doormat

Baddies

after the MGM slogan

It should be said for the sake of it
There is no better reason I think
For thoughts to make a break for it
Like convicts from Her Maj's clink

My only hope's they're sympathetic
An Eastwood, Clooney, Pitt or Caine
The loquacious gangster's copacetic
That gives the slip the lawman's chain

Or said not seen, the greatest heist
That springs the mind's own Alcatraz
And steals away the thoughts we diced
With cell-block tango razzmatazz

This sleight of hand is our diversion
It breaks the rules but keeps the line
And dupes surveilling self-aversion
To think each passing thought is fine

For when we judge, we jail, are jailed
These sentences commit offence
They section us where none are bailed
Their terms betray our innocence

Head Hunter

after Takin' Off (1962)

Ha! I'll chop in your head
and like a Foley artist infer
from a lick exploded tact
the watermelon propped
and Dexter's laughing axe

Social media

It arrived after the naming of it, late
Again – the first denuded conker skull

Scouts out the pristine lawn
As birds do windows.

Thud go the swallows, thud the verified beasts,
Thud, thud, the mellow fruits on each our houses.

It's only me   they say   *hello hello*
In bucket-loads from Birnam Wood

Sorry I'm late   how time flies   how are the kids
I'll see you soon, darling   Goodbye, goodbye!

So occasion fledges the sound from its wings
& plonks like so the knock-mark of a harpy.

Lines on the Greenwich Fault

May 7, 2020

When is evening ever like London skies in the water
guising sun – there, and there, a thousand times there –
like mayflies, mooning busily along the wide-long mirror
lifelong farewells that lapse bedward, between the Thames
dockyard and the seven sleepers barricading the invisible
horizon from its daily autumn, whose burning valley splits
headfirst the cloud-spill grey, like a slow-shredded wing,
west of the mudflats, as east the Moon if you could see
him, moulting wildly across the slick, melting the surface
in double image from outer space caught now in dawn –
or like dawn – from the sugar factory, where I am, to the O2
obscuring fault lines, where continents were elsewhere
raised, but here crease invisible, unimaginable, beneath
the wharf in Reminder Lane, across the yellow warning
signs, the twisted scaffolding of a trolley, a child's play-
thing, the street along an empty pier, and under it
the yawning sewer, the forgotten dead, the toll on a paper
boat on a daily redtop – while evening sweet, distended,
sets too our soulless course, and calls it tomorrow

How to be a poet

after Milton

An honest poet knows good and bad,
Finds Satan squat atop his knowledge,
Buys him a drink, checks out his pad,
Writes verses praising him in homage

But leaves off rhyme (it's overrated),
He soars! Then falls! Repeat. Emetic.
Then goes blind, lives mostly hated,
Solitary, divorced, and areopagetic.

He makes up words, is sensuous,
Can turn god-fearing angels pink,
Calls pinioned sex less strenuous
(Like air, we'd mingle as we think),

He reasons reason is but choosing
That thought's divine and not for all
When knowing's freely disabusing,
What makes a thief's heretical.

Fible-fable

A vision of a dream, or fragments from a nonsense epic I was unable to finish – for sanity's sake

We three vultures merry with wine
    Perch hunched in our communion;
Together we dine on the beach and the brine
    Altered by night in our union.

Dogstar, bless us! for we are drunk,
    The fool in us presides:
Our wings are clipped, our mouths red-lipped,
    No feathers dress our sides –

Never has gravity been such a bother,
    We curse our depressed state –
Like a tumbling pigeon that's eaten a smidgeon
    Too much to bear its own weight,

I find myself quite grounded, on
    Account of being unfit,
As if in spite of previous flights
    My wings from wit have split.

O! What a state to find oneself,
    Uncouth and like an ape;
To travel bipedal is so unregal,
    How I loathe this flightless shape.

See how we've sickened preying on morsels;
    So long we had fancied a change.
We dreamed of matters beyond corpse-platters
    Metaphysical and strange:

A paradise of perambulation,
    A menagerie of men,
A land for walking, a world of talking,
    Penned in acumen.

We knew it out there to possess,
    Having read the figures below,
But our bird's-eye view did misconstrue
    The matter wholly so.

Calamity (for although we gained,
    Our loss was greater still)
Did weave from nothing reams of nothing
    A fibre prone to pill;

The defect fabric of our fate,
    Our baseless, knotted dream,
Was not what we had thought our lot,
    No knot, but knotless seemed.

Seems? I know not seems (we said)
    It is – we are – for sure!
The cause of our grief is to be solved in brief
    With a slight altercation in form.

Piffle, piddle, claptrap, crib,
    Bibble, baffle, boo,
Fible-fable, apple-babble,
    Dapple, soddle you.

To Autumn

And is that all, and
All that's left of me,

Bare coat-stand scarecrow
Like a mugger in the hall?

Say I mustn't go. I will not satisfy
The gleaning walks of Morden.

Take my hat, scarf, boots and coat,
You'll do a fine impression.

Yes, I'll stand here stock-still
Like a decommissioned tree.

Nobody will tell the difference,
Not even the best of them.

Acknowledgements

Firstly to you, for getting your hands on this book: thank you—and oh how kind!—for sharing it on social media. It's the least you could do, since you're nosey enough to rifle through my literary receipts, like some grubby gossipmonger.

Aaron Kent, James Riding, Suna Afshan, Lucy Diver, and Molly McDonald, clearly you are meant to be here. Thank you. Likewise friends, family, mentors. Consider yourselves truly acknowledged. Also, too, my enemies, who I cannot name for legal reasons but blow raspberries at nonetheless.

Diolch, *Poetry Wales*, for originally publishing 'Dating' and 'Shave and a Haircut'. And finally, to everyone at Broken Sleep Books, for this—the room, the microphone. Solidarity.

LAY OUT YOUR UNREST